whiskey words & a shovel I

whiskey words & a shovel I

r.h. Sin

Andrews McMeel
PUBLISHING®

thank you Samantha, my baby.

and so it happens, nothing is the same.
everything altered by overtrusting
and believing in someone who fed you
beautiful lies, when all you ever wanted
was the truth. this had been my biggest
problem, a major issue in my life.
investing all of my hopes and dreams
into someone who never actually meant
the things they said, someone incapable
of keeping their word, and I'd only come
to find out when everything had already
begun falling apart. there's this slow
collapse happening around you, but
you're blind to it because you hold on to
what little hope you have left. looking
back now, I should've known better. the
red flags were all around me, but I was
blinded by a love that was tainted and
promises that later revealed themselves
as empty.

I was searching for peace in the middle
of chaos. I was searching for a love
in the midst of hate. I was promised a
lifetime of understanding yet I stood
face-to-face, constantly in battle with
the person who should have helped me
fight off sadness. I let this go on for
years, I stayed when I should've left,
and I'd continue to fight and not be
fought for. there I was, thinking it
could never happen to me but it did. the
slow burning of everything I built upon
a foundation that was sand, washed away
by the floods of deceit. damaged at the
point of betrayal but after I healed
myself. after months of ignoring phone
calls, refusing to respond to "I miss
you" text messages, I found my truth and
discovered a greater love for myself.

it all begins with you, everything
and anything. it all starts with
you. I realized this to be true as I
continued to self-care, more aware of
what I wanted, needed, and deserved.
on December 3rd, in the middle of the
night, I received a message from a young
woman named Samantha King. I fell in
love with her laugh over the phone on a
Saturday evening; I fell in love with her
eyes and her smile over a video chat. I
fell so deeply in love with a stranger
who lived in New York, thousands of miles
away from me. on the 19th of that month,
we'd go on to become a couple and with my
second visit to New York months later to
meet her, I'd end up staying.

originally, this book was released on
the 25th of December 2015, and it fills
me with great pleasure to share this
updated version with you. this list of
events, summed up in the form of poetry
and prose. my past is yours, the present
is ours, and the future awaits us all.

thank you Samantha King for being brave
enough to let me in. I write to you
in thanks, not only as your partner
but now your fiancé, someone who is in
desperate need of your existence and
presence for the rest of my life. in
these pages, I tell a story of pain,
but in my life, next to you, I am
overwhelmed with joy. you are proof that
there is good waiting for anyone who has
lived a life of pain. you are proof that
soul mates exist and that they can be
found even in situations where one has
given up hope. I'm so happy that I found
you, or maybe you found me. regardless
of it all, you helped turn my grief into
happiness. you helped turn my nights
into morning once more.

notes to the neglected ones I.

young girls neglected by their
fathers

forced to grow up

like plants without sunlight

without care, without that love

and so they search for that love

in the arms of boys who are incapable

of loving them in ways

which they desire

this urge to be loved romantically

created by books, movies, and music

filled with fairy tales

far from their own reality

boys pretending to be men

promising love to young girls

who are not yet women

young girls broken down

first by their fathers

then by boys who will one day

be completely irrelevant

but the pain that they cause

will somehow manifest itself

as something greater than

they'll ever imagine

young girls weighed down

by the weight of things

they should have never had to
experience

life events that should have never
occurred

but they did and they will

young girls neglected by their
fathers

forced to grow up in the coldest
conditions

this is a note to the neglected souls

notes to the neglected ones II.

no one taught you

to love you

and that's your biggest problem

searching for validation

in people who will never

accept you for you

being made to feel

like you're not good enough

trying to prove yourself

to those who will never

be good enough for you

taken away.

who robbed you of innocence

who told you things

you've never heard

who made empty promises

swearing to God

that they'd do something

they never actually intended to

who was your first

who took your virginity

with meaningless compliments

and a love that wasn't genuine

who made you feel things

your heart wasn't prepared for

who fooled your heart into falling

I'll tell you who

the same person

who later abandoned you

after getting what they wanted

the same person who pulled

at your heartstrings

with the intent of playing you

like some horrible symphony

and the saddest part of it all

you'll cling to the good memories

as if there were any

you'll take these dirty walls

and paint over them

with the brightest colors

known to man

but the pain will always be there

can't be life.

sadly, so many people

are setting the bar really low

in terms of their personal lives

working a job they hate

content with struggling

settling for relationships

that aren't actual relationships

life for so many is not living at all

and that's the problem

you get what you allow

watching others live life

instead of living your best life

and they wonder why everyone

is self-medicating

suppressing their pain

pretending to be happy

instead of trying to cultivate

a lifestyle that brings them peace

with lightning.

she is a storm

a magnificent force

writing her life's story

in lightning

14kt.

woman

you are a poem

written in ink

derived from gold

painful roots.

you planted seeds

bearing dishonesty

and pain grew in my heart

start to finish.

this is the part of the book
where shit gets a bit weird
you're reading this to yourself
without the realization
that I am now talking to you
directly, until now

repeat after me and this more
than once if you need to

I am grand
I am powerful
I am electric
I am incredible
I will survive this
I will be fine

understand yourself.

you are the light

that most men

will never deserve

silence tales.

she could tell stories of hurt

with silence

her smile was broken

so was her heart

and yet I still knew

she was perfect for me

truth of self.

to be honest with myself

I was never what you wanted

I was just the one you settled for

2417.

try, fail

try again

fail more

I just wish you could

have fell more or feel more

death knocks on our door

eviction notice and I'm hurting

which is why I wrote this

our story, our book

I'm done reading, time to close it

if love trumps all, then why the hell

is he our potus

and if I'm overrated

then why am I the most quoted

been valuable all my life

but none of my lovers seem to notice

and so it's fuck love, claiming I'm done

but I don't mean it

true love exists

it's just that we don't ever see it

self-sabotage

it's like we do it to ourselves

but I'm through like needle and thread

when I was just trying to help

no words.

silence says the things
we struggle to say

the experience.

you're an experience

more than a woman

you are lightning striking earth

your presence is electrifying

under stars.

meet me here

beneath the stars

near the moon

in the dark

I've been waiting

for someone like you

you are.

I know you

you're the girl with the broken smile

you're the woman who searches the
night

for peace

you're the woman

most men don't deserve

you're the woman

someone needs

infinite us.

I assure you

that when this life ends

I will find you in the next

no matter what the circumstances are

our love is forever

everlasting, never-ending

out of hurt.

your words

sound like hate

when the heart

is hurt or angry

split.

you were never the one

this was never love

and we were never meant

to live happily together

you were simply necessary

I had to be hurt by you

in order to find my strength

my hope for you.

and I hope you find
what you're looking for
more love of self
and someone brave enough
to lose sleep with you
holding you in the thickness
of the night
when you're restless
I hope you find the love
that you deserve
and spoken words
that'll make you swoon
a hand to hold
and lips to touch
first thing in the morning
when you wake up
I hope you find the truth
and nothing less
something that'll bring you peace
something that'll make
your heart smile

first day of February.

your child is not a weapon

your child is not some tool

that you should use

to hurt others

it hurts my heart

it tears me apart

to witness your inability

to appreciate the efforts

of those who only wish

to love your child

as if that child was theirs

your child is not some weapon
and yet you use this child
in that way

not realizing that you're only
hurting yourself
by destroying the bond
shared by others
just to protect your own

the control.

and that's how they control you

they make everything appear impossible

they force you to believe

that you're almost average at best

they force you to forget about your
magic

and with this, you forget about your
worth

we are more prone to accept a little

or nothing as opposed to having it all

we're content with small sums

of what will add up to being without
value

in our last days of life

our desire to achieve more

has been buried beneath

the ideals set by those

threatened by an above-average ambition

don't let them control you

don't let them define

and or set your limitations

just be.

woman

be strong

be educated

be opinionated

be independent

you will only offend

the weak

you will only frighten

the closed-minded

and you will never

be appreciated

by those who don't

deserve your presence

and that's completely fine

similar foes.

no matter the gender

no matter the sexual orientation

no matter the color of skin

we are all haunted

by the same emotional devils

we are all running from similar
demons

but you're used to it.

you're so used to being mistreated

that you allow your heart

to remain in dirty hands

you've gotten so used to being hurt

that happiness scares you

into staying in a relationship

that will further break your spirit

put your phone down.

social media

has made us less social

we observe the lives of others

instead of living out our own

dreaming instead of doing

liking what we see

while hating what we do

all nothingness.

limitations self-imposed

choosing to conform

to the idea

of not having your own ideas

we work to further the agenda

of others

neglecting our own dreams

to labor behind the efforts

of helping people

bring their dreams

to a reality

content with being the worker

sitting below the boss

content with being a spectator

with minimum participation

our version of living

feels more like death

as we pretend to be satisfied

with nothingness

fifteen.

I sit here in a dark room

on the 15th floor

the rain beating at my window

the city skyline

becomes my nightlight

as I type these words at 11:13 p.m.

on a cold Wednesday night

my heart breaks at the thought

of you reading these words

with a heavy heart

my heart breaks because

you most likely picked up

this book because your heart

is hurting

I understand you

I see you without seeing you

I feel the scars on your heart

like braille

somehow reading the stories

that often go unread

within the pages of your soul

mother of pain I.

insecure mothers

jealous of their own daughters

chipping at their self-esteem

attempting to kill their dreams

young girls forced to survive

into womanhood

18 years old

the age at which

they can finally escape

the death grip of an insecure mother

mother of pain II.

daddy's girl

abandoned by her mother

everything she's become

given to her by a father

who filled the void

that her mother left

12:16 after midnight.

I was forced

to survive

in your absence

I was faced

with the realization

that I never needed you

days.

you're always apologizing

for the behavior that'll never change

one day I'll stop listening

one day I'll stop believing you

all but nothingness.

we grew apart

we stopped trying

we were no longer us

we became nothing

processing.

I'm trying to get better

at walking away

from unhealthy situations

involving my heart

winter begins.

come winter

a cup of coffee

and a woman

with a free spirit

is best for you

child within.

the child in me

will never forget

the pain of being left behind

by the parent

who was too selfish

to stick around

silent thought.

forced to feel like

my all was less than enough

I struggle with the idea

of anyone loving me unconditionally

t.b.h.

sometimes I wish you waited for me

instead of wasting your efforts

on temporary distractions

until I arrived

I worry.

you love people

then betray them

how am I not

supposed to fear you

after you claim to love me

how am I not supposed

to question your loyalty

when you've cheated

on people

you said you loved

found in solitude.

I'm attracted to the silence

of your absence

at first, the fear was loneliness

but I found my peace

being away from you

insanity driven.

women are made

to appear crazy

by the very men

who drive them

to a place of insanity

fed up.

to be totally honest

I got tired of going through

the same shit with different people

we're guarded.

guarded because I know betrayal

guarded because of lies

guarded because of pain

guarded because my love

is not for everyone

connections.

connect with someone

who makes time

to connect with you

earliest lesson.

my parents taught me
that marriage means nothing
when there is no honesty
loyalty and effort

0722.

marry someone

who complements your soul

among stars.

every night

the stars

envy her

every night.

girls

like you

deserve a love

that makes

it easier to sleep

during the coldness

of night

midnight noise.

nothing is louder
than overthinking
after midnight

never ready.

you weren't ready

for someone like me

and I had to accept it

final departure.

I left you

I walked away

you had so much potential

but refused to use it

his issue, not yours.

it's not your fucking fault

you can't change a man

you can't make a man

love you correctly

that's not your fucking job

understand that most men

won't know what to do

with a woman like you

and that's okay

you my dear

are not for everyone

blind and confused.

I think it started

beneath the false sense

of security you provided

I was manipulated

into trusting you

unable to hear the lies

that at first presented themselves

as the truth

the thought of being in love

is blinding

the thought that I'd found the one

filled me with so much confusion

and I've been struggling

to find my way out of this

first or many.

he was your first

you were one of many

my eyes ache

witnessing girls give everything

to boys with nothing

my own whisper.

my mind whispers

to itself

all those lovers

but none of them

loved you

full of emptiness.

maybe the heart cracks

to empty itself of things

I no longer need to feel

and it's become obvious

that I no longer need

to feel for you

same phrase, same results.

and so she thought

that it was love

but he'd used those same words

on every broken girl he met

taking what he wanted

giving nothing

leaving them empty

modern barter.

bargaining using sex

either way

you get screwed

hung up, hung over.

I've been growing impatient

trying to survive on empty

your promises were like rope

wrapped tightly around my neck

the chair beneath my feet

the only thing holding us up

<u>hers.</u>

some silence is loud

year 2008.

I remember what you don't
I recall what you refuse to
I fight, you sit and watch
I yell, you tune me out

everything we are
became everything we were
our love, fractured
broken beyond repair

wet works midnight.

midnight nears

and the moon shines

its light

directly toward my pain

and so

I'm unable to hide

my phone in hand

as if I'm holding on to hope

awaiting your texts

anticipating your call

as if to prove that I matter

to you

it won't happen

a thought that sounds like a whisper
to my heart

a pistol aimed at my head

bullets made of disappointment

penetrating through my smile

a smile that I originally thought

was bulletproof

today was difficult

and tonight is equally the same

as my body trembles

under the weight of my own heartache

midnight nears and I'm alone

with the moon

regretting the day that I allowed you
in

some whiskey wordplay.

so many men

fear your strength

and the fullness of the waves

in your ocean

so much they'd prefer puddles

and that's fine

the pain in remembering.

the memories hurt the most

they destroy bits and pieces

of our existence

draining us of our energy

keeping us up at night

sometimes I get tired

of thinking about the things

I don't want to think about

sometimes I get so fucking tired

of everything that reminds me

of you

1 a.m. restless, always.

these memories are silent killers

the way they creep up unannounced

disguising themselves as innocent

knowing damn well

they intend to cause harm

and if that's the case

tonight, you'll be the death of me

under the moonlight.

I remember lying there, quiet

fading into the silence of

our four walls and a window

that gave permission to the moon

as it watched us from afar

thinking to myself

you can't force someone to realize

that you're what's best for them

the illusion of good mornings.

she was his morning coffee

enough to keep him awake

until he found someone else

to consume with his bullshit

my energy misplaced.

loving you was draining

instead of wasting

my emotional energy

I decided to forgive you

and move on

mountains underwater.

mountains submerged by water

dreams drowning, promises scattered

at the bottom of the sea

a reversion of my rights signed

and now my soul feels free

a California lie.

screaming bullshit

until my voice gives out

and silence is all that is left

a mountain of dreams

still in boxes awaiting transport

under siege by friendly fire

people I used to trust

the ship carrying me begins to flood

the ship carrying me

now sits at the bottom of the sea

the ship carrying me was too weak

to hold my dreams

the captain was a fraud

he could never match my drive

I am safe in New York

no more California lies

something for this night.

tonight won't be easy

and you know that

I know it hurts

but the pain is necessary

everything meant to break you down

will build you up

and you'll become stronger

a broken beautiful muse.

broken, I cut myself trying to help
you

piece it all back together

your fragmented heart

on the bathroom floor

the door was closed and I could hear

you weeping even as I was sleeping

curious to the sound

awoken by your efforts to hide

what you could no longer keep hidden

broken, yet as I looked into your
eyes

I saw strength

we were different people after that
night

beyond your past.

come

allow me to help you

bury your past

let us give life

to our future

past and present.

constantly

I'm always moving on

you're always coming back

leaving for long lengths of time

only to reappear

when you fear you've been replaced

the never-ending cycle of what we were

the constant mistake that we've become

now cold.

it was your love

that caused this

it was you that made me

this way

suddenly being heartless

was better than being heartbroken

being cold was better than the warmth

you failed to provide

all of us.

all these people

with pain in their faces

bruises on their souls

and cracks in their hearts

we have found ourselves

trying to survive the death

of what we thought was love

fighting to make sense of a reality

that is now a lie

it's easier said.

sometimes I wish

changing my heart

was as easy as changing

my mind

good hearts.

the only downfall of having

a good heart

is that you find yourself

constantly searching for angels

inside of demons

and they wonder why the good

know so much pain

devoured.

devour her the right way

and her back will rise off the bed

she'll bite her lip

and her thighs will shake and
tremble

devour her the right way and she'll
begin

to flood the surface of your lips

and the sheets on your bed

snowfall in Queens.

oh, how the snow

makes the cemetery

look alive

the heart vs. the mind.

I hate it

the way the heart

takes too long

to figure out what the mind

already knows

this peacefulness.

first

I missed you

then I learned

to live without you

I found comfort in your absence

I made peace with being alone

memories in midnight.

midnight belonged only to us

she was always down

and I was always up

she on her knees

willing to motivate me

watching my own funeral.

you were the death of me

no wake, just a funeral held

in memory of the person I was

before you deliberately destroyed me

forcibly making me a victim

in your path of destruction

what was there to love

nothing is what I've come

to realize

but only as I lie here lifeless

screaming but not being heard

reaching but you refuse to reach back

I now know that I was in this alone

my relationship with you

now my casket, a tomb

awaiting the burial of the person I was

gift of the broken.

it hurts but I find myself

pretending to be fine

"I'm okay" has become my favorite lie

and my smile is usually a mask

that hides the truth in what I feel

I'll say nothing because

you'll think I'm weak

I'll say nothing and let

my silence speak

the gift and curse of the broken

being able to hide behind lies

of happiness

the gift of being strong in a moment

of weakness

easier but difficult.

it's easier said than done

is a fucking excuse to stay

with someone who doesn't even care

about keeping you

let's be honest, I know it's difficult

to leave behind the person

you care about

but shouldn't it be harder

to hold on to the person

who doesn't care about you

the all of nothing.

all of those friends

but you're always alone

whenever real shit occurs

all those lovers

but you don't even know true love

all those bodies

but nobody's there when you need

them the most

all of this is all of nothing

November 22nd.

she's full of pain
but filled with fight

before any proposals.

the idea of getting married

scares me

but not in the way you'd think

my fear stems from realizing

that I am truly alone

and that I'll have no family

in attendance

my fear is in being reminded

that I have nothing more to offer

than myself

and throughout time

that has never been enough for anyone

including my family

sometimes mirrors lie.

I don't really recognize

the person I've become

a year can change a lot

it has seriously changed me

restlessness.

no more losing sleep

over someone

who can't even find time

to consider me

going to sleep

because you no longer

deserve my thoughts

the afterthought.

and so it happened

I set fire to every memory

we'd made then smiled

watching us go up in flames

his last resort.

I think there's something sad

about the fact that he only reaches

out to you

so late in the evening

in his own way admitting

that he could care less about you

with each passing hour during
daylight

horny and bored

he chooses to pursue you

in the evening, under the moon

under a blood moon.

stuck in the gaze

of the blood moon

its red eye shines

its light on me

and I am ashamed

for I have given in

to your pleas

and empty promises

I've given up on myself

by giving you another chance

to hurt me

I'm trying for you.

I want to dance with you
but my knees have been bruised
and weakened
by all the moments in my life
I spent kneeling for a prayer
that consisted of my desire
for someone like you

I'll fight to hold your heart
even though my spine
has been weighed down
by a life of despair
and disappointment

how brave is it
to love completely
as if you've never been hurt
and though I've been
an emotional wreck
I'll try for you
because you're worth it

fragments.

I tried

you left

stay gone

from start to finish again.

just when I've reached my end

you return

expecting us

to begin again

the burial site.

and so I suppress

these feelings with whiskey

I bury you with my words

then cover what we were

with dirt

<u>using a shovel in my journal.</u>

sometimes nightmares are people

staying away means staying awake

being alone brings me closer to peace

surrounded by bars.

you've become like prison

I'm planning ways to escape you

midnight, often.

the morning rarely comes

stuck in a constant loop of darkness

the moon my only friend

I've gotten used to the silence

that surrounds me each night

closing my eyes, trying to forget

I remember everything I don't want to

I've been hurt more than I'd like

trying to remain strong

my knees weak

from the weight of it all

my nights are war zones

at midnight, I go to war

when angels fall.

angels fall to earth

forgetting about their wings

holding on to things

they should fly away from

pride in brown.

my brown skin

will not be a burden

my brown skin

will not be my enemy

I love me

regardless of their hate

no entry.

I burned our bridge

then built a wall with no door

many maybes.

maybe your arms

were too short

to reach me

maybe your heart

was too weak

for mine

I struggle to comprehend

your inability to love me

as much as I loved you

cracked glass.

you don't see how beautiful you are

because you're relying on a broken mirror

she kept dancing.

the ground beneath her shaking

the foundation she stood upon

began to crumble

unbothered by the destruction

she danced like flames

at a bonfire

icy roads in Pennsylvania.

roads paved in ice

we slide calmly

through the snow

our backdrop

an empty white

the forest reaching inward

branches stretched toward us

as if to hold our hand

guiding us to our destination

even in the most dangerous

of conditions

we are safe

hopeful romantic.

I assure you

that when this life ends

and the dust settles

I will find you

in the next

no room.

do not let temporary people
and the sadness they bring
make homes out of you

necessary evils.

I believe you were

simply necessary

I had to get hurt

by you

in order to find

my strength

after ruins.

I reached my breaking point
every part of me fell apart
sitting here in ruins
I'll rebuild without you

these words I.

I think I'm just trying
to write away my pain
as you turn the pages
in this book
you're reading away yours

these words II.

you're reading this
with hopes of finding something
that'll give you a peace of mind

you're reading these words
in hopes of settling the dust storm
that has been living in your soul

I hope you find your clarity
in my words
I wrote all of this for you

witnessed.

I've seen women fight

I've seen women break

I've watched women fall

I've witnessed women

pick themselves up

I've observed women

be everything and still get treated

like they're nothing

and even through all of that

I've seen women get through it

I know it hurts

but you're strong my lady

you're going to be fine

confusing.

he loves you

but hurts you

he misses you

but never shows up

I get it.

you're not happy with him

and I know this because

you're reading this now

while questioning his commitment

my own value.

I began to see the true value
of my own heart
this is when walking away
became a bit easier

loving you meant
that I didn't love myself

control yourself.

men are often using the words

"I miss you"

in an effort to manipulate

a woman's emotions

remember this always

open your eyes.

when you read the words

"I miss you"

pay more attention

to the actions that follow

instead of allowing your heart

to feel things

for the person who at one time

broke it

know and understand.

the words

"I miss you"

will always sit

upon the lips

of the man

who tried

to break you

but failed

imbalance.

the most loyal hearts

are broken by betrayal

a solid regret I.

never make a woman

regret investing her trust in you

a solid regret II.

today wasn't easy

tomorrow will be even harder

I've accepted my fate

my punishment for allowing you

to reenter my life

without good reason

your hidden motives

and bad intentions

revealed to me once more

after you took what you wanted

leaving me to feel empty

and filled with the regret

of believing in you again

share this with him.

listen, she loves you

she adores you

be more considerate

of her feelings

be more understanding

of the things she expresses

because if you were to lose her

you'll have lost everything

perfect match.

more than anything

my heart longs for

a lover who will always

appreciate my worth

and match my effort

a real man.

has a man ever asked you

if you've eaten today . . .

has he ever given you a compliment

without expecting anything in return . . .

has he ever congratulated you on your
achievements

and pushed you to aspire to do more

has he ever claimed you as his queen

not with words but with his actions

has he given all of himself to you

to the point where

he could never share anything with
another woman

has he ever done or said anything
sweet to you

not because you asked but because he
knows

that you are to be treated like the
queen you are

have you ever had a man be consistent
in the positive treatment

that you've been longing for

does he make you smile even without
having to do a thing

have you ever had a man who is afraid
of losing you

because you are that valuable to him

this is a real man

have you been with a real man . . .

dirt.

buried alive

under my own

expectations

heart rate.

the pulse of my heart

has been screaming

for you

a standard.

treat her like you're afraid
of losing her to someone else

search party.

I am trying to find myself

under the rubble

of my own heart

the mind, her eyes.

talk about her mind

compliment her eyes more

she's too rare

for average compliments

1:04 a.m.

everything is poetry

when your heart is in flames

11:11 p.m.

she wants a man

who doesn't want

anyone else but her

dried up.

we were roses

slowly dying

fighting to bloom

summer '11.

searching for something

to numb the pain

I'm tired of pretending

it doesn't hurt

the death of an indie.

I was wrong about you

hiding a mountain of lies

underwater

but the truth always rises

to the surface

true colors.

it's funny how much a person's

true colors shine

after they've gotten

what they wanted from you

exhibits.

watching you in the museum

is like witnessing art

observing art

savage.

the heartache made me
so fucking unforgiving

note this.

in you

lives a love

that most people

won't be able to comprehend

hate the process.

it takes too long

to realize

that they're no longer

good for you

challenge.

hashtag

stop wasting

your time

on him

a tweet.

you're way too valuable to be in a
relationship with someone who has
proven incapable of understanding
your worth

living in denial.

do not live in false hope

you can't find love

in places filled with hate

just stay.

I'm just a fucked-up lover
searching for someone who
will understand my scars
and never leave my side

thirty-six notes.

it hurts

and I just want

to stop thinking

about you

fifty-six notes.

it feels hopeless

and yet you're still

hoping for something

that'll never happen

reading regret.

you're the chapter in my life

I should've skipped

2007.

I hope those lies
burn your lips

pain to remember.

we've become a set

of memories

I'd like to forget

distorted.

our relationship

a room filled with broken mirrors

I barely recognize myself anymore

deadly habit.

my most dangerous habit
is overthinking

pillars of salt.

you were salt

hiding in a bag

labeled sugar

all in the end.

this was never meant

to work

I was holding on

to nothing

I'll dig deeper.

the parts seen and unseen

the portions of you that require me

to dig deeper

appreciating every inch

of your existence

there are several layers to a woman

and some men are simply stuck

on the surface

but I'd like to learn you

discover my rightful place

within your mind and heart

allow it and we'll begin

see I'm no longer who I was before

my mind under construction

growing closer to completion

as I transition to a place

where I'll have the opportunity

to explore you

and hold on to everything

that those before me

were willing to walk away from

I'd like to love every part of you

that those in your past were too
blind

to acknowledge

the parts within you

that they failed to appreciate

allow me

no fun.

drugged by the culture

you struggle to fit in places

where you don't belong

you struggle to understand people

who don't deserve your effort

innocence robbed

by the party scene

loud music

drinks flowing

surrounded by all these people

and yet you still feel alone

you're only here

because your friends

wanted to go

in fantasy.

that's the problem

you're living in a fantasy

that involves him being

more than he actually is

you're in love with a dream

that will never become a reality

because he refuses to be

the man you deserve

genuine love.

love me when things are bad

love me when the storm arrives

love me when I've lost all hope

love me through my imperfections

willing.

the heart is broken

but the heart is still willing

and that's what makes you strong

the essence.

sweetheart

you're a star

never apologize

for burning too bright

wet Marie.

with two fingers

a few strokes

she began to overflow

and I was willing to drown

for her

demolish temptation.

she knew I was taken

she knew I was in love

she offered up herself

but I declined, I said no

see, pussy can only sway

a weak man

strong men refuse to stray

my love for my lover

is so much stronger

than anything anyone else

could ever offer me

more.

she's not easily impressed

shallow compliments

have no meaning

it takes a bit more work

to flatter her

she needs more

she deserves more

2:30 a.m.

I think the heartbreak

changed the temperature

of my heart

your lies became more like bricks

which I used to build this wall

the barrier that sheltered my heart

and kept my love safe

was also the very thing

that kept new love

from getting in

the whiskey fights.

I yelled because I actually cared

I only argued with you

because I gave a fuck

and now I'm silent

nothing left to say

no more fight in my heart

this is when you should worry

more consistency.

I demanded consistency

and you consistently destroyed

the best parts of me

I guess I should have been

a bit clearer

about what I was asking for

alone now.

no one wants to be alone

and so they find themselves

in the company of someone

who makes them feel lonely

there is loneliness

in being with the wrong person

the brave.

she wore her scars within

beneath her skin

and you'd never know

her pain

as she's chosen not to complain

being hurt, being silent

having courage as she fights

through it alone

so much strength in a woman

so much strength within you

inconsiderate.

young woman

do not compromise yourself

for someone who refuses

to do right by you

overly entitled.

a lot of men feel like

they deserve everything

from a woman

who deserves more

or someone better

I wonder.

what happened to actually

making an effort

for the woman who

continues to prove

that she has your best interest

at heart

the good man.

I care about a woman's
experience when she's with me
I care enough to ensure
that being with me
feels easy and secure

how could you not care
about the impression you leave
with the woman you're with

love and excuses.

love should have never

been a reason

to hold on to someone

incapable of loving you

many devils.

but sweetheart

you're an angel

don't let these devils

undress you

the nights.

each night

the same old shit

you wait up for a call

that'll never come

while he misses out

on the opportunity to speak to you

I know it's hard

feeling the way you do

I know you're restless

lying in bed

while reading this book

but remember the next few lines

in this piece

you are strong, intelligent

you are worth it, you are beautiful

and you deserve so much more

than you have allowed and accepted

July '15.

I once heard that the tongue

gives life

and so I spoke into her

flames within.

there are flames

within my soul

so deep where no water

can reach me

and I continue to burn

I enjoy the sensation

even though it hurts like hell

pieces of peace.

it's amazing

the way your broken

gives me peace

you've been hurt

and yet

you're still able

to make me feel whole

without judgment

I accept you as you are

scars and all

imperfections visible

you're still beautiful to me

a search for love.

so many angels

are going through hell

in search of love

dating demons

temporary highs.

you were only meant to be
temporary
I wish I knew this before
I spoke you into my future

the slow death.

slowly, death crept up behind me

and as my grip got tighter

holding on to you

was killing me

the book of ashes.

together we wrote the book

on our relationship

and tonight I'll burn the pages

deserving more.

you always end up trying

to please someone

who isn't even satisfied

with themselves

you're constantly searching

for a love within someone

who doesn't even value themselves

you've been wasting your time

holding on to someone

who doesn't truly care about

keeping you

the great wall.

maybe she built that wall

in front of her heart

in order to save herself

from the pain she's become familiar
with

maybe she's protecting her heart

from anyone not willing to climb

that wall

to claim the love

which she refuses to give away

so easily

into the chaos.

I followed my heart

and it led me straight

into the chaos you always were

I nearly lost my damn mind

the lines.

there's just something

about her

the type of high my mind craves

she's the feeling of late nights

after hours on Fridays

she's my good-time girl

whenever I'm stressed out

she helps me cope

like an actor doing lines

she's always been my coke

the inside.

her tears

rarely visible

the sound of silence

as she screams on the inside

scars and bruises

in places you'll never see

often overthinking

filled with words

she'll never speak

going through hell

she'll never tell

she has a guard up

refusing to believe

the bullshit stories

her man tells

not forcing.

I can't force you

to be faithful

loyal

and honest

I can't make you

appreciate everything

that I am

but I can force you

to live without me

as I invest my time

in someone better than you

the life lessons.

through relationships

I learned that someone

who is yours

can never be taken away

and if for any reason

you lose your lover

to someone else

that person never deserved

to be claimed by you

moonlit.

you're the moon

just lying there alone

you shine in the darkness

your power

is in the night

this moment.

somewhere

right now

someone is searching

for everything

that you've wasted

on someone

who never deserved you

everything that you once thought

wasn't good enough

will one day be appreciated

by the one deserving of you

vanishing.

I became a ghost to you

you missed me

sometimes you felt me

but you could no longer see me

I've learned to vanish

from those who fail

to appreciate my presence

some whiskey with dinner.

the truth was no longer

on the menu

and love was no longer

being served

this is why I left the table

I'd rather eat alone

all the little things.

if you don't love the way
her eyes squint when she smiles
or the way her lips curl up
whenever she's filled with laughter
stop wasting her fucking time

still beautiful.

you're not perfect

there are scars

on the surface of your heart

I'm convinced that you've experienced

a set of painful events throughout

your life

as you've become

what people refer to as broken

in my eyes, you're the most beautiful

arrangement of broken

I've ever witnessed in my life

looking at you, thinking to myself

there's my future, she's the one

fear of falling.

my biggest fear

is having my peace of mind

compromised for a person

who is comfortable

with telling me lies

my heart placed in the hands

of someone who refuses

to meet my demands

settling for a love

that feels more like hate

these are the things I fear

and yet I find myself

playing with fire

making mistakes

claiming it all as fate

until I find myself in love

with someone who causes

my heart to break

I fear loving the wrong person

and so I choose to not

love at all

and that's the scariest part

possibly I'll never fall

fake care.

I dread the winter

not because of the weather

solely because of a person

my peace interrupted

by the troubles that live within them

silence transforming itself

into tension

me wanting to get away

while they fight for some attention

I should be excited

but I'm not

I should be happy

but you've robbed me

of that very thing

being forced to share my space

faking a smile on my face

because that's what good people do

sacrifice themselves for others

but I'm tired of being that person

I'm tired of being the one

from distance.

I can love you
but only from a distance
some people are more lovable
when they're not around

our love 22.

I love our solitude

we live in this peaceful bubble

we've cultivated a garden

filled with roses

that bloom, nurtured by our peace

our silence gives me comfort

this is easy

this is us

sin-ergy.

and just like me

you're a sinner

I'm your accomplice

on your knees

against the wall

on your back

I'm always there

a reminder.

just because you're broken

doesn't mean you're not beautiful

a moment of weakness

doesn't define your strength

the perfect aim.

I'll walk away

and I won't miss you

this .45 fits perfectly

in my hand

and my aim is so much

better than it was before

some optimism.

it hurts like hell

every minute of every day

but it'll get better

one day you'll understand

that everything meant to destroy you

only made you stronger

masks I.

there was something so damn special

about you in the beginning

you were rare but time revealed

the most honest parts of you

it turns out

everything about you

was a lie

and you were just like the others

never a loss.

at the end of every day

I find comfort in knowing

that I've only lost the people

who never deserved to stay

poetess.

you walk around here

with your head in the clouds

writing about a love

that never existed

a love claimed by a man

who only used the word

to get what he was after

you, calling it a relationship

when all he did was

stick around just to sample

what he'd never truly commit to

taking all of what he could

before leaving

this is the reality

of what you claim is love

great regret.

in all seriousness

I thought this was real

I believed in you

and that's my greatest regret

before and after.

I am no longer

the person I was before

I allowed you into a place

untouched by the hands of anyone

before you

I held the door open

just so that you could walk in

and make a home out of me

you took my willingness to allow you
close

and destroyed the walls of my heart

you took the trust that I gave you

threw it away as if to say

I wasn't good enough

before you, I was different

after, I'll never be the same

constant.

that's the problem

you're constantly

searching for heaven

where only hell exists

you're constantly

searching for peace

within a place

where chaos resides

you've been expecting love

from the same individual

who offers

nothing but hate

hope kills

when invested

in the wrong relationship

she, flame.

she was the flame

that no one could put out

burning brighter than the sun

refusing to be taken lightly

she was driven by

all the things that caused her pain

and what failed to weaken her flames

became fuel

she is you

I want you.

show me the woman

with scars on the walls

of her mind from overthinking

cracks within her heart

from loving the wrong person

pain attached to her soul

but I'll fight for the chance

to love her

a woman like her.

lying there

wearing nothing but regret

eyes swelling with water

as if her heart

was being sunk

flooding, slowly going under

midnight has rarely

been kind

to women like her

forced to relive

what would become

a major mistake

in trusting someone

with pieces of herself

far too valuable

for most men

but no one knows

until it's too late

and sadly, the truth

only reveals itself

in the end

forcing the soul

to be filled with

so much resentment

and tonight is just like any other

a woman with regret

a woman fighting

to get past whatever it is

that keeps her from smiling

and somewhere amongst the pain

is a silver lining

because women like her

always find ways to survive

deep within.
---

your strength

is your magic

never lose it

emotional hostage.

he kidnapped her heart

held it for ransom

took what he wanted

with no intention of loving her

the reasons why.

and that's why she stayed longer

than she should have

because it hurts to watch

something you love

transform into

something you hate

she sits and waits for it

to return to its original state

in denial as she ignores the fact

that what she sees was always there

limitations imitations.

we could have been great

this could have worked

but you insisted on being mediocre

you placed limitations on us

so I chose myself

I chose to move on

knowing that I deserved more

<u>my theory.</u>

you can't keep a man
who doesn't deserve you
this is why they leave
this is why they rarely stay

some word porn.

she wants to be taken

mentally starved by a mind

incapable of stimulating hers

my knowledge and understanding

like food for a dying soul

I became the only thing

she could think about

rooftops, lying wide-awake

and vulnerable under the bright moon

in lust with the way I speak

my open mind

opening her up

every word, like a thrust

or stroke as she invited me

to spill my words on her canvas

letting go entirely.

maybe that's all she wanted

acknowledgment

to be appreciated for all the things

she did

someone who cared enough

to make an effort

the type of appreciation

that could be felt

a man who could love her

in the same fashion

as she loved him

I don't think she was asking

for too much

all that she demanded

was simply what she deserved

you served her a bunch

of lies

and expected her

to get full

starving her of the truth

but one day it happened

the woman whom you

only wanted to break

reached a point where she

could break no longer

though you thought

she'd hold on

she finally found the courage

to let go

passive-aggressive.

I'll sit in silence

I'll say nothing to you

but if you continue to

place me as a secondary concern

you'll lose me without warning

she's an artist.

she was broken

but somehow

she found peace

in the pieces

scattered across

the floor

she's an artist in the way

she pieces herself

back together

to create something stronger

and a bit more beautiful

than before

one of those days.

it's almost as if the sun is

peeking through the dark clouds

I should be happy

but I'm not

lust under moon.

I don't think it was actually love

I was just obsessed

with the way you made me feel

on satin sheets

under the moon

June '15.

what was meant to be

a celebration of sorts

sadly, now feels more

like a funeral

the transformation.

I was more in love with

who I thought you were

and I hated

what you became

reaching.

open your eyes

don't be blinded

by your heart

stop holding on to someone

who is obviously reaching

for someone else

losers with benefits.

the fucked-up thing

about using someone for sex

is that you're probably

being used just the same

by someone who doesn't deserve

a portion of anything

you have to offer

using them while wasting yourself

pretending to win

yet constantly losing

crown me 722.

she crowned the tip of my head
with the lips between her thighs
my Queen made me King

your sharp tongue.

lies like razors

you claimed to be

telling the truth

yet I watched you bleed

from your mouth

Sin's choice.

realizing that I didn't

have the courage to love you

in the way you needed

I let you go

because you couldn't

I did it for you

pitch dark.

after the sun has set

and the moon decides

to present itself

after midnight is when we

often remember

the things we try

our hardest to forget

December 22nd.

you are the most beautiful

type of broken

I've ever seen in my

entire life

and though your heart

is in pieces

you deserve to be loved

and I'd like the opportunity

to be with you, always

an observation I.

the women who smile

the most

are often the ones

who experience

the deepest pain

she doesn't wear

that smile to deceive others

she smiles because

it's a symbol of strength

often we pretend.

please notice

the sadness in my eyes

but if you ask

I'll claim to be fine

an observation II.

maybe it's because you're strong

maybe you hold on

because you're capable of

loving him unconditionally

and maybe he's just too weak

to appreciate it

the wound.

completely broken

I cut myself

trying to get close to you

several attempts

I almost bled out

for you

us, our future.

come here

I'll help you bury

your past

we'll give life

to our future

a sober thought.

I've been missing you

more than the usual

either I'll run out of bullets

or improve my aim

that's where my head is at

walking toward the future

I've lost count of how often

I took you back

the morning after.

it happens

you wake up one morning

and the feelings

you went to sleep with

are no longer there

you picture life

without that particular person

and instead of feeling worried

you begin to smile

what you felt continues

to fade

Sin's request.

I want everything

he took for granted

I have this desire to explore

the parts of you he neglected

but first I'll work for it

everything within you

is not to be given easily

but earned

repetitive.

found pain

searching for a love

you couldn't deliver

distance between self.

you know, I've been losing me

for a while

my reflection appears partial

as I often feel less like myself

and further away from the person

I'd like to be

my truth.

in all honesty

I never miss

what I walk away from

there is no regret

in walking away from someone

who gave me a reason

to leave them behind

burning bridges.

I'm the one who burns bridges

just to light my path toward

a better direction

I'm the one who uses failed
friendships

and relationships as stepping stones

toward my future

under skin.

her scars, invisible

she was hurt in places

no one could actually see

lustful and lust filled.

our love was weak

passion only exchanged over the
strength

of a climax experienced in the back
seat

of a vehicle or on the floor

next to the mattress

we rarely slept on

body talk.

in a sense

we rarely talked

communicating with our bodies

the arch in your back

told me everything I needed to know

journal entries.

it has always been easy for me
to get a warm body in my bed
but finding someone
who deserved to lie next to me
was something I struggled with

your painful truth.

you pretend that it's love

because the truth is too painful

and being alone is unbearable

shortest story.

he moved on

she stayed there

waiting

afraid to be alone

though loneliness was all

she'd ever felt

while being with him

no explanations.

hurt me

and I'll leave

without warning

I don't owe

an explanation

to those who mistreat me

love of self.

one day your love

for self

will outweigh the love

that keeps you holding on

to someone who chooses to hurt you

one day the love of self

will be your strength

that love will be more

than enough reason for you

to walk away for good

the next.

I don't grieve the ending

of any of my relationships

because I know what's to come

will be better than what I've had

a restless soul.

it rarely gets easier

the late nights under the moon

restless, unable to retrieve peace

slowly losing yourself

so far from who you were

and though it doesn't get any easier

you find yourself strengthened

by the pressures of the world

your potential.

you were everything

I should have avoided

but I stared into your potential

instead of paying attention

to our reality

the truth is, you were never

the one

and I can finally admit it

view finder.

I think I got tired

of looking at you

through pictures

I was eager to double-tap

you in real life

same thing again.

it's always hard at first

good mornings aren't possible

most nights are spent

digging through the rubble

of your own anguish

sadness swells and turns into

bruises

today is just one of those days

tonight, it'll all be the same

the 17th of December.

light snow falling

outside my window

your head rested on my left arm

my eyes fixed upon an imperfection

on our ceiling

I'm a bit nervous because

in two days

I'll drop to one knee

possibly two

asking you to spend an eternity

on this earth with me

my heart rate increasing

as told by my fitbit

my palms are sweaty

drenched in silence, overwhelming

and now my dry lips

whisper "I love you"

my heart longing for our future

your head rested on my arm

so full of love.

submerged by you

like ice cubes

drowning in whiskey

I'm in need of everything

you have

I'd like to be wherever you are

the midnight motion.

I am tired, restless to say the least

my eyes heavy, refusing to close

sadness weighing down my eyelids

but not enough to see me sleep

the moon stares at me

watching from afar

as I break off into the night

like the sun setting behind the ocean

cold air fills the sky

matching the temperature of my heart

love escaped me once again

pain is all that is left

my bones aching

under the pressure of depression

heartache mistaken for insomnia

the only cure would be to dream

but I'm alone, here beneath a full
moon

unable to sleep

close to the reaper.

the closest I've been to death

was lying beside someone

who had all of a sudden

stopped loving me

our room like a tomb

killing ourselves while holding on

to the nothingness that we became

I did this to myself.

I've committed a crime

on my own soul

mistaking you for the one

mistaking your lie for truth

unable to see this for what it was

blinded by potential

in love with love but never you

what we became.

the greatest lie we tell ourselves

involves a love that is tainted

and a relationship that becomes toxic

strangely beautiful but broken.

I saw the flaws

and devil paws

imprinted on your heart

cracks caused

by being involved

with a demon selling dreams

and telling lies

to capture your love

used and abused

then left near a curb

next to day-old filth

overwhelmed with guilt

and an ocean of regret

your would-be grave

as you fought sinking

to the bottom

the broken woman

as labeled by others

would soon become

the woman who made me whole again

all of everything, you are.

strong, unapologetic, and free-spirited

everything a man like me

everything a man such as myself

has been looking for

here, this moment.

and maybe, just maybe
we'll look into each other's eyes
and see our future, together

my heart has been longing
for someone like you

where we end, for now.

the day is December 18th

the year is 2016

and I woke up next to

the most beautiful woman

in the world

my muse has loved me

and I have loved my muse

this book in its entirety

would have never been possible

if it weren't for the support

of Samantha King

healing the wounds

left behind by my past

giving me new life

new hope as she's loved me

in recovery

whiskey words and a shovel
documents my highs and lows
your highs and lows
our highs and lows

this book is a literary documentary
of what happens when love is tainted
and what could be
when love is pure

thank you Samantha King
for encouraging me
thank you for being the lighthouse
to my ship

here's the funny thing

I associate Samantha King

with a lighthouse

because she's been my guide

she has helped me navigate

the chaos that had once been my life

and tomorrow

the 19th, I will get down on my knee

or knees and ask her to continue this
journey

with me

no matter how broken you are

no matter how tired you feel

no matter how weary your soul becomes

there is someone out there

willing to love you completely

but you must first love yourself

with whiskey

I buried my emotions

with words

I once lied to myself

pretending to be okay

telling everyone that I was fine

when I wasn't

and with a shovel

I took all of the pain

I had experienced at the hands

of someone who pretended to love me

and buried it deep

in this series of books

I dig up that grave

in hopes of helping you

find clarity and peace

I love you Samantha King

and thank you to the readers

until the next time . . .

index.

whiskey words & a shovel I

Andrews McMeel Publishing
a division of Andrews McMeel Universal
1130 Walnut Street, Kansas City, Missouri 64106

www.andrewsmcmeel.com

ISBN: 978-1-4494-8806-2

Library of Congress Control Number: 2017934705

Editor: Patty Rice

Designer, Art Director: Diane Marsh

Production Editor: Erika Kuster

Production Manager: Cliff Koehler

attention: schools and businesses